LOVE IS COLDER THAN THE LAKE

LOVE IS COLDER THAN THE LAKE

LILIANE GIRAUDON

TRANSLATED BY

SARAH RIGGS & LINDSAY TURNER

NIGHTBOAT BOOKS
NEW YORK

Copyright © 2016 P.O.L. éditeur

English Translation Copyright © 2024 by Sarah Riggs and Lindsay Turner

Originally published as *L'amour est plus froid que le lac* by P.O.L. éditeur

All rights reserved

Printed in the United States

ISBN: 978-1-643-62197-5

Cover design and interior typesetting by Kit Schluter

Typeset in Futura PT and Garamond Premier Pro

Cataloging-in-publication data is available from the Library of Congress

Nightboat Books

New York

www.nightboat.org

IN MEMORIAM R.W. FASSBINDER

It's not enough to hold a book in your hands to know how to use it.

—ACHILLE MBEMBE

... for I am making it not just possible on the stage but demanding the stage ...

—STÉPHANE MALLARMÉ

I

LOVE IS COLDER THAN THE LAKE

. . . there is no psychological state behind it,
because when the poem is done, the poet is dead.

— KEITH WALDROP

deliver the coincidences

                          the angles the sounds the stars

dead but still visible

like us

are you hungry
are you cold

turtledove   come back

                      come back sing at my window

what is "fast"

An atmospheric pain   The life I live   The book I don't write
    Alone between the tower and the hangman   He did say atmospheric   All
that is family history   Mineral lineage   Something even more
fundamental and repugnant   Block rose lilac   Cyclamen close to grape
Making a relief   In the surfaces of greenery

of the enlarged carnivore

orchid or café au lait same difference

the shape of the water

so that's why Macbeth assassinates sleep

for example
                    to get stepped all over
to have had enough

she says she mistook the coat for
the skirt no
a man doesn't wear one

nothing ever replaces nothing

I could go bicycling
                    nothing doesn't exist

Love-Hate that can be done   Some do   The book is our
book   Each minute of each morning   A plumbing treaty   Sometimes
a blackbird sings   Poor sweet things   Sire it's a very beautiful perfume
*   Like everything that flowers together   Among clusters of dried blood*
*   White of the white night   The rose ridge   Silence lapping*

stuff his ass with paper

you can strike the matches with your thumb

next time don't tire yourself
send a monkey

deadly fragmentation or perennial variety

Greece seems to melt
                              easier even than butter
the blows of the Persian Empire

the darkness is great

The system's modalities belong to a voyage's   *Lost also*
even if bunches   Naked girls in Kodacolor   Antibiotics and
chocolate   We cry we laugh   You remember then you forget   Pastel reflection
on all the acts   Take your time   Drink some Schnapps   Screw
your mothers   Chat up your cousins and your brothers' cousins   Eat some
mussels eat blood sausage   It's still summer hours

           alas   AHEAD OF TIME

it's printed above

you will return
             you promise

like the war   The famine

somebody knocked something over
                                        someone picks it up
the invention of ruins was in fashion that year

nothing is no longer anybody

We were dancing   You like to dance   You dance well
   Who is it   Why do you look at him   Let's take this outside where I can take
care of him myself   I had warned you   I'll take down the next one who touches you
   Dirty whore   Dirty little whore

today is tomorrow

to wreck the pronominal form
I would like to work at it
                              like eating petits-fours
peel an orange or squeeze a lemon

in anger   No
we are not angry

the mess on my table
whether I eat or I write
in perfect harmony with my thought

raw beans to go with the evening pastis
                    + Emma Goldman in fine form

nothing to do with me
                    I row
in search of holes

The more she remembers the less she feels present   It's a rare experience
    A simple child's   Bastard a lily without a label   Of the torn
sheet   Some drops on the skin   A single little bowl   I love who
loves me otherwise not   Sire don't go thinking that I'm lying to you   The
kingdom is inside the bottle   Far from Orpheus sodomite widower

stellar language fallen in the lake
                    some men-women-frogs
seeking the wrecks   a theoretical fiction

invisible declensions in the direction
                    of the animal reign when to torture
the living isn't enough

on set
nénufar is no longer waterlily
nor spatterdock

clothes clean and hanging loosely on the line

the grandfather was part of it
from a network he helped the slaves
                          flee toward Canada

The disappearance of ritual is a new form of ritual   The question is asked
    Today it's fashionable to say that books don't change anything   But I
tell you   To read changes everything   We are talking Reality   We are your
    Contemporaries   To read is to live   It's a war machine   A
porn star   You are the subject in question   A bird in the hand is worth two
in the bush   Open our books   Sleep in your clothes   Make love standing up   Dig
your graves   The sun has risen   The moon stopped in its place

all the animals
                     irradiated should have been killed

now they proliferate

in Italian in the original version the title
male role is held by a contralto

all the musicians smoke in the film

Orpheus warbles as coxswain

modified in Paris
the contralto became countertenor

she declares
"Gluck was an accident"

the distances must be reinvented
                              fuck it all up
be afraid no longer
                    from the evening or the rising morning

those who eat their excrement are stronger they
have vanquished the whole
                          of the interior fears

This inside which stinks and sickens   You must be able to bring it back to the
light   To throw it in the lake   To forget everything that turned us away
from the sun one morning   A puddle in the bottom of a bowl   Yet simple
to understand   Get out   Leave your women and your children
*   Drown them   Cut their throats   Go on vacation   Get the hell out*

of those ones we can say that they
have lost the foundation
                          an unchanged animality
all hot air

or else a saffron-yellow shirt
                    torn under the arms

he carries her by derision
or simple sadness
                    the days where to die
would seem reasonable

when art occupies
the shelf of aberrations
                        the theory of signals

becomes a child's game

no one eats anymore
                    no one drinks anymore

the grotesque has overcome all the rest

this suits our work perfectly

For what can be seen it's enough to stamp   Then to move to the back
of the garden   Below not far from the youngest fig tree   Continue
what had been started   It's very simple   For the treatment of all
the voices off-screen   A finger seems placed on the lips   The screenplay
ends with   Thank you for your visit and see you soon

pretty fast the presence of speaking bodies
opens the series

the infection you cured with what
                              a little coarse salt
the whole tube thrown into the water

he says no it just happened
just through crying and waiting
                    stretched out there without waiting for anything
not from life really or from anything

the women especially who always
had wounded or betrayed

To start with his mother whom he hadn't known   Had left him on the ground
one summer evening   Not far from a passenger station   One would think it
was a bad novel from the last century   Shared cruelties   Memories screens
Bonus: a still dragon   Placed in the center of the image   While under
the mountain of clouds   Orange sun with almost green reflections

I no longer keep a journal
I no longer draw
                    what is happening

without a single word

he says now
                    my slumber is deep
the sleep of a bird who knows
                    the forest its turmoils not a breath
between the trees but everywhere in the air
some bits of slogans

and you why do you never respond
to the real questions

we might think that's a dog barking

a car passes one of them remembers
                                        others move a plate

The little artichokes in a glass jar   As if they were
flowers   That could be charming   Living completely displaced
Delicious although also distressing   She knitted her hat   She says
she repeats   At the end of the act she is slapped   It's written in the stage
directions   Everyone has to slap her   Before jumping out the window

Mephisto combines all the characters at once

Snow White rots on her feet

she is mushroom but it's the apple
which sticks poisonous
                              in the deceased's throat

the children's slipper found after
the accident he says I kept it I could not
throw it out I am sure that the child is dead

how to show what's off-screen in the poem

when going becomes necessary
                              to work the voice place it each
evening each time you open your notebook
                              sun or lamp middle of the day
early morning double choir
                              of the birds from the other side of the lake

In a Sade play   A tiger metamorphoses into a young man
   Very pretty young man   Whom the marquis names Lili   A
cream-colored gauze cravat very voluptuously tied   A little lace
ruffle   For the marquis iris powder   Elderflower eyedrops
   Chervil poultice   Foot baths   Application of leeches

it's not a girl
                     more like a panther
it's a boy
           who has a girl's name

you have to proceed to a test

at times the remark is analogous
to the reasons

I no longer entertain myself
I no longer keep myself company
                            cutting my toenails
becomes difficult

Some evenings   The critic like her sister   Must define the impossibility of the theory of reflection   It's he who gets the inertia moving   Making clear that technical agility doesn't have to hide itself   Beneath a clumsy exterior   At the indicated time   The shades detach from the bodies

we note the numerous accommodations
for violence

hunger misery death seem
always necessary to the proper functioning
of the State

we work on it it's obvious

open the door let
                  in the ghosts
here intervenes
                  the legend which includes
all the photographs

the decomposition process
of our existences
they say they don't give a damn

it came

like a glass of water
in five columns and without indentation

The story of the stags in the forest   Bury under real branches   What
is the meaning of this apparition   Saying at night I make piles of logs   I
dream that I pile up logs   It requires incessant attention   An
incessant attention   Don't go thinking it's funny   Every morning
I wake up   Exhausted

Faust's destiny embodies the destiny
of the bourgeoisie the horror of that class

those we have the right to kill
and those we don't have the right to kill

in Shakespeare already
we find all our everyday

make it so that
                                some are killable

*Do you eat horse   Some birds   Your power of existing is it
strong enough   And your wife   Have you sufficiently penetrated her   Is she
satisfied*

but what's it about

*He says he'll come back when everything is finished   That nothing will be possible
anymore   Since it's the poet who surveys   The spiritual door
opening onto the Third Reich   While far away the night begins to
fall   Violent   Wild*

a submission
impassioned by the object that occupies it

when one of the victims recalls
                that to realize is to vomit one by one
the anachronistic pages

to realize the whiteness of the cod

to be pragmatic then see what happens

like Molloy calculating the average
time of his farts

to act she says "I want to act"

everything turning liquid means
that everything happens
to liquefy someone means
also to kill the person

the dislocation of the world
the true subject of art

*We will no longer go to the wood   I should learn to be quiet   The day is
sad because the departure lasts   The territories are clearly drawn   The
dream machinery   Facing interactive consensual abjection   A concept
that does everything   As was said about maids   Room under the roofs
     With neither water nor electricity   If the service is too long   You will
wear diapers   We will deduct them from your salaries*

the communal body
it'll get cold again

she says mayonnaise
instead of fresh butter

repeating in love I am a little colossus
tracking the ambiguous rhyme lower down
dampness of brain the same and the opposite

a concept of the lake
added to that of the crack
random identity of the sirens
                    LZ great predator
disorientation in scales

one and the same fishbone
                    LN displaced functions at a loss
a germinative conception of letters

"paean to place"
                    a poetics of the cannery

Sweet life my love   Have you ever tasted this delight   The marrow
of the bone   Don't be afraid of spilling wine on the cabbage   I saw a star
whistle before falling   Under a proper name a common name   Something
backlit   Lost in the grass   She says I learn to condense
   No layoffs from this condensery

the words auto-braided each night
hair white that's to say dead

"exception made unless"
seven years the same dress
torment infested with shadows
                    taking books and chrysanthemums

24

the question of form in language
           how to live it while making it
           fusion and confusion
the virus is an information
logic of transparency

she says a nation without State
           it's possible look at the Roma
transnational minority spread
across territories of many States

tzigane gypsy
that means Un-Touched

here is a white

missing a page
           without a doubt torn off

the next day

           he says he won't come back

We don't need words   *They bury them alive up to the neck*
  Then they smash their skulls with spades   *This additional*
act is called   *The flower*   *Psychic close-up*   *A partial visual object*

the sun swam in a red
sauce not a breath

in case of catastrophic emergency
everything will be eaten cold

they say that the retina is too hard
you have to displace the lens

incise your arm Faust
                    show a little courage

I hear the sky which moves

damned be the one who flies
                    the meat of its holiness

the only winning move is not to play

Don't leave us   Keep your hand in mine   Do you remember
how much we have suffered   Since they separated us one from another
*   These times are not so far   To find the pure event*
of the image   Its living currency   It would be so difficult   Bite into
a body as raw as a turnip you would dare

that they come in a profound silence
                    and then they leave

let's stay here or there
                    the place doesn't matter

when the evening falls the heart
tightens a point set lower down

and that a finger enters

systematically tar black
for the notes at the bottom of the page

substitutes in images
                    instead of concepts

have you forgotten the shrimp-pink
of the duvet that covered his bed
the crushing fierce yellows of the air

Series of parables in successive waves   We don't believe our eyes   We don't
want to believe it   Yet the things are there   In the shade of the trees   At
the base of the walls   Sometimes buried under skirts   The infection goes around
It spreads   Invisible   Effective   Lewd

all the muses stricken
                    with Alzheimer's

and these floating black clods
                    surfaces added to terrible voices
each night
                    you had forgotten them

a chaise longue
a simple chaise longue
sheltered from the wind

some material elements are added
to the formal elements

for example bitter orange
                              or camellia other times just
lilacs in static bunches

On the doorsteps   The angels eat jam   Wipe while
singing   They enjoy the fresh air in clear weather   Kiss full on the mouth
between two Te Deum   Declare to whoever wants to listen   God is a rat
who cons you all

an unreadable draft
and riddled with holes

here for the readers and the bean chant
                              old delicate kindred language
with candied ginger

with Dog-Poem truffles
 damp and fresh for some
                              she might just end up rotting the syntax

a soundless oratorio
                              all the work is for the eyes

before reading look at each page
as if it were a puddle

The Furies: ferocious cocksuckers   Armed with torches carrying whips   Their faces   unseizably beautiful like oysters   Their buttocks are flat   Some sleep together   Their step is quick   Frightens the pregnant sheep and the grasshoppers   We still sacrifice to them today   Some narcissus   Saffron   Occasionally hawthorn

in their eyes a general picture
of forms of flexing

sometimes the teeth are discovered
before and in front of
                    up high down low and outside

the immediate nasal falls

blood flows

                    the desideratives
express the desire to place
                    the act indicated by the verb

they bite and they chew
                    so that the bites become
visible on the flesh of the passersby
                    the operation can take years

for a long time the three sisters
looked for Vivian Maier in Chicago

simple reflections in a mirror

often she wears a hat
                accompanied by the children

The use of the stolen portrait   Combined with the undeveloped negatives   Erases
all traces   Still we'll get her back   The stubbornest boy of all
A larger form of the son she didn't have   The nurse-photographer
becomes the stage actress

brief syntaxes perspectives
slow mobile excavations
                but we advance vertical
depth something thick
                not really
                black atlas of use
the terrible infinitesimal surface
its intimate exterior

the Furies wouldn't have known
how to scan in high definition

we must return
to the notion of failure
                    Faust's sex life
the fact that Hitler loved stories
of Indians it was all he read as a child

repent
the demons are going to smash you to pieces

she suspected it

She says she suspected it   *That she always preferred the margins to this*
stamp of the avant-gardes   *Branded*   *Like a cow*   *No she*
says I prefer not   *She says*   *You are miles from imagining*   *What*
can excite me

come back Tuesday for the co-optations

today it's cheese without dessert

in rhyming verse   and in Latin
                    you take yourself for Catullus
                    and you are but a cretin

I stand by what I said
it's Faust himself who will train
Marlowe in this seedy inn

in clear weather with relative ease

there where he will die assassinated
yes twenty-nine years old
who   Marlowe or Faust

don't be stupid I saw you piss
                you've eaten asparagus

The vowel carried over can be dropped   In certain cases I did say
certain cases   And these cases will be rare besides they have disappeared   we'll
end up renouncing dropping the vowels carried over   Then all the
others   We'll drink for consolation   We'll smoke weed   We'll shit
in the plates

pure gluttony will extinguish language

olfactory memory: it works
                like a muscle there that's why
we forbid children masturbation

the beauty-pageant anthology
                aiming to form a local bureaucracy

she says you have to break the tool

every precise form
assassinates its precedents

here we should introduce the titular lake
                              it's a character
love will wait
                              like all assassins
it knows its time

the eye of the lake decomposes
it's a paradigm

I've enough of being treated like this   *No man's ever spoken to me*
the way you do   I can't take it anymore   I want to die   Get out you
destroy me   You have destroyed me I can't take it anymore   I should have
listened to my father   My mother my sister   My cousins

stop confusing emanation
and analogy take a bath
                              go to the movies

the order of words is free
                              the order of lakes is aleatory

here's a statement that will cost you

an altered voice
not necessarily articulate

like the lambs' voices
just before the throat is split

It seems that she had been practicing self-beheading   *A mysterious*
art   *Invisible to all though carried out daily*   *Often*
in full daylight while everyone looks on   *But who cares for what*
actually happens   *The thing you tell us is clarifying to understand*
      The rotten existence of all the actors   *Here I mean of the life of stage*
actors   The destiny hardly enviable to which they're condemned

it was in another life
                         at least all not the whole story
was invented for often
                         he'd invent stories
about the women he had ceased to see

the word "raincoat" was used
three times

when she embroidered with electric wire
                         the dresses she made the youngest son wear
it was always during a storm

the water temperature
                can be variable

the question of relations of force
                will come up incessantly
all throughout the notebooks

these become a material artifice
like most uncertain things

the one who wrote them is dead
                but the notebooks are today's
or the ones who live today

like Vivian Maier's portraits
or Twombly's peonies

Variety just as vivid the sun on our heads   *When I left the book it*
was daytime   *A sunbeam rested on a leaf*   *The youngest of three sons had*
managed to grow   *The mother's body was decaying at the bottom of a pond*
    Nothing noticeably crude or failed   *Among the tufts of grass*   *Hardly*
showing at the water's surface

this evening they beat to death
a sixteen-year-old boy
they did it in a cave
                        his body was found
a shopping cart in full daylight

he was still breathing

Darius first prince inaugurated by lynching
premonition of a new form of pogrom

The transformation of an experience into language   Bestial manifestations
of a compensation   The story is of water crushed in a mortar
*   The problem with the dead is that they never complain   Stop*
bringing it up   Go out get some air   Water your flowers

wedding of blood
                        or mating of shit
persistence of murderous consent

a fertile vocabulary
heads move the arms

opposite meaning
                        when to give form is to form

we'll pay attention to it then forget

drying her tears he told her
I wish for you to be kissed often

Friday the 13th contaminates the week

counterpoint: the true legend
of photographs of reality

it is a tempest that blows from forgetting

bring in the fruit bowl it's going to rain

Perhaps it is a question of desire   In the middle of the petals   Poppy-red under
the oleander   Back when I didn't know they were poison   Daisy
pollen or spray of light   For the broom blossoms in the omelette
* We had warned you   It's not the day and it's no longer the time*

the story like the story
                    of the sufferings of the world

that "petal" should be masculine I just can't get used to it

otherwise

another desire
                    in shallower water this time

distinctly

the boy says he sees
                    a dead man sitting close to me
I see the dead everywhere
                    he says I see them
as I see you

I prefer them to the living

they never lie

the words seek
>   to hide the sentences

in response the sage
flowers why not write
with your shit like painting
>   with blood why heat wave

shave a head coat it with petroleum
some have done it some still do it
>   total incapacity to calculate the profit-limit
of cowardice

like believing
>   in instruments and in stars

what interests me only
>   is what's not mine
it's what the other repeats
>   but everyone knows he's lying

When texts illuminate lives   A swallowing of differences not
the opposite   For example to make something unexpected happen   Good evening
it's me again   You're going to think I'm crazy but I begin again   First
you are going to suck my cock   And tell me you like it   I know you're
there so pick up   Bitch   Pick up

since the epoch is a lake
                    we have to look elsewhere

the bloody haze
one morning a pigsty at the site
of the camp the chapter of the ignoble
                    stays open to the same page

a line of writing and who is speaking
uncertain a hardly foreign language
he says and repeats often but not really

                    when to read becomes a way
of listening to what the voices say
                    of the lake compact series unpaginated

in this context the voyage always precedes
                    an explication of the map

A night's dreams add themselves   The key in the water   She says
now I no longer distinguish the night's and the day's   I am
a filthy beast   In the northern forests amid the birches   They say
that when an animal is dirty   It's because it's sick

optical work
            somebody else's life dreamed
by a third

*Vivian in a low-angle shot declares herself a spy   She doesn't give a damn who
interrogates her   Double-locks herself in her borrowed bedroom
    Piles up journals   We know nothing about her sexual life   Nor about
her feelings*

that she cuts up   her fury her secret

when he uneducated by the birds
doesn't know that the woman he penetrates
            each night is his mother

victories of detail the self-effacing messes
form open bifurcations

here history repeats itself it's boring
persistence of deadly consents

in the mountains the man in yellow socks
walks with steady steps
            smokes and speaks in gothic

the Roman empire an epidemic
Theorem and *Saló* one
and the same film

manual work
                        for the most afflicted

in the guise of punishment
the market key to the pleasures of the body
or drugs a new way
                        of articulating time

daydreams of the lake

discovering that Hölderlin
imagined in his Song Notebooks
SS officers crying

in blinding reflections
                        rumination

The most exact practice of writing the poem   Walk by chance   Exit
by strong wind   To stride the roads the alleys is only a pretext   An
old mania   He takes the child's bloody face between his hands
   Screams he never wanted that

all is open
but everything empties

                        the margin is the center

when the young girls were in flower
it was the false essential character of the useless

lower down
the techniques of fulfillment

degree of proximity
with the spheres of power

today September 21
                it's autumn

Bits of voices rising on the leaves   *Planing-Light-Return*
    Where have they gone the arbors full of wild roses   *It was*
another century   *Another world*   *Useless to leave yours to*
find it again   *Air-conditioned*   *Anti-theft locks*   *Cell phone*
    To each his tweet   *It's now*   *It's nerve-racking*   *It's funny*

each yellow sock of the man
who smoked and spoke in gothic

the crusaders swallowed
children on a spit
                    did you know
since then we have done much better

fuck off with your civilization thing

intersection of causal series
                    which is to say a continual lighting

as he had read Brecht well he recommended
"distancing" over "detachment"

why I write

anonymous serfdom including me

here the lake smokes
                    it's dawn without history

At the bottom of the screen   Return of the body of a swan named Mallarmé
*   A monosexual version   Simultaneously designating the political   The mass*
grave we put out   The observer is part of the observation   He needs
his dose he needs it

when to slap or be slapped
one and the same stain

new forms of immersion

forcefully specifying
we cannot repeat it

she is dead she is really dead
     the desperate penultimate always
already completely forgotten

without fear of disorder
the side effects make themselves known
      with conviction one day I dreamed
that I was my brother and my sister

Adding to produce the right legend I'm working on it Like riding a storm
When the lake is calm   All the birds went quiet   I sing
alone   Under the clouds   A gorgeous moonlight envelops
* All the riverbanks Roll of sequins in shining metal This praise*
of precision takes on a new significance

as usual she exaggerates

if we read the *Oresteia* in fits
of a matriarchy ending
     the whole film lightens

the one who can no longer sell himself is subaltern

in reverse-angle
dying out the people moved

devoured vesperal column neither meat
nor fish gillyflower berries stand up straight
a little pat of butter on rice

auto-itching for each syllable
                    the real world becomes a useless function
the eagle flying over the two columns
                    adds his memory to the cicada

I was a woman I was a woman

A delicate and watery menagerie   The sun and its white love   On
the green leaves Lorine goes into   Otherwise   Oviparous mammal
varying from one translator to another   Poisoned immune movement
*   The lost child replaced   By a dog   Rather small   Who was castrated*
and whose vocal cords   they made sure to sever

if I'm it doesn't matter who
                    inter-laking on the lake she traces
another line spreads
                    the space between words differently

a two-way psyche

                    what's dictated

when we call her
she answers that she doesn't answer anymore

dark spite
against knowledge this love
images enlivened by a pronounced taste
for whispering
                    ceaselessly occupied

when the norm requires obligation
                    little matter where the wind comes from
or if the man can't kiss

Traumatic present's incessant command   *Today Jocasta's*
a pedophile's wife   *While elsewhere*   *On a tabletop*
   The listless swan's yellow feet   *Ideal instrument*   *For showing*
the poem's histrionic truth

the extra speaks elsewise of something else

the only response to drama
                    practiced even if new
the modest observation
                    of movement in the trees

here a return to the man
who smokes and speaks in gothic
his name is Cingria

                    Charles Albert Cingria

to wander to roam
                  never to stay put
just as the setting stays cold
I will stay cold

it's what he imagines

a projective geometry

victory of details
                  or simple survival
a learning of life

When Latin persists beneath language   *The girl turns away*   *Absent from*
history   *Doesn't understand*   *You know I don't think I'm hungry*
   You should really eat something   *Dreams are always*
circular   *I have an atrocious migraine*   *You think you can get out*
   But you are here and it's now   *Take off your skirt*

lake of love without waste

                a synthetic anus

he recommended that she
take the time to laugh

                or breathe

as a response she sobs
into a paper tissue

a draining-out between the paragraphs

                there's no metaphor

only conjugations

an experience

                of emptiness between the words

To each his community   Jockey-club of the avant-garde   Rank-and-file of
the rear   The art of making a balloon into a bomb   Lumpfish roe
into caviar   The trees' massive bodies all lying down the same way   We
won't be betrayed   Nor tortured nor shot down   We are artists

everyone has lost their teeth

only polemical modesty remains
little ordinary works
handwritten lines & nocturnal drawings

what's deposited doesn't belong to anyone anymore

Remember she who recommended destroying the negatives   *Denounced*
    printing as an anesthetic apparatus   *How post-mortem*
the husband trafficked the manuscript   *Air-conditioned*   *Anti-theft*
lock   *Halogen lights in the big cities*   *She accepts the cigarettes*
offered   *Often goes out alone at night*   *Finds pleasure with*
women

because we are tired
                    because we are disgusted

a supple approach in the background
the changing botany of death

half-ray of the minute when
the page supposedly white
is crossed like the lake
                    a celluloid bather

here there is no why

just a little salt
                    it disinfects you'll see
                    you won't hurt any more

dream it at night
like drops in the eyes

body
element of intrigue
                    and of space

the child says mama when we die
the blood stops flowing
yes my darling the heart stops also

the market deals obedience
                    it normalizes disobedience

to see to know to understand
becomes full-time work

When breathing becomes difficult   *Just pour yourself a double*
    Light a little cigar   *She takes off her glasses*   *We see her eyes*
ringed with lack of sleep   *She passes a hand through her hair*
    A little red almost black   *It's funny*   *It's morbid*   *It's*
sexy   It's now

she doesn't say that in less than a year
                    skin and flesh will disappear
only the bones will remain

laugh you have to laugh

because a fabric's defined by its weave
where you put the links
                    of the "homemade" poem
like a pie or a casserole

slaughterhouse chops up
                    the factory assembles

It's clear   The majority of fiction films begin after
the workday   Free accumulation of associative stuff   The oxygen
masks will drop automatically   Please   Make sure your seatbelt
is securely fastened   Your tray table folded   Your salmon fresh

what she writes
                    about poetry
yes but problematically
and without the slightest guarantee

can each being be his own historian

when the images of war
                    say nothing of the war
that pornography reaches
                    the most chaste embrace

I liked it so much when he put
his two hands on my hips

evening didn't ever stop falling

simple fruits of a constellation

montage in counterpoint
all the bodies interlocked occasions
                              of intrigue still supple
but not reconciled sighs
                              some words but never
a whole sentence or a cry

mountain setting overlooking the lake

only violence helps
where violence reigns
                              it's an old song

half wild half lost
she invents the poem's backroom
                              its marginalia

how to show it
visually

Go back in up to the waist Out between the holes   *Without fear of*
 currents   *The brutal wind or the trees uprooting*   *The deep dark*
To stray from the bank is to never return   *This isn't a*
game   *Higher stakes than play*   *The rent paid what's left for food*
They'll fish for carp   *Cook scraps of fruit*   *Caress their girls*

Antigone turned Creon assassin
isn't that enough for you

somebody else's life dreamed
                              by a third

a feather in your ass

*Going around repeating   The decline of handed-down experience   we don't
give a damn   Those who are born today will see the earth burn   I see it already
I sense it   They walk on bodies   Everything is said   We can take them
at their word   They cling to it   If you're an artist   Brown gleam
   Apricot   Your work is to offend people   Grate to the bone
   Pretty things soft in the night   Gentian secrets   It's not for you*

like through
                    layers of tracing paper

living I descend into the savagery of the dead
                    repeating Oedipus's child

the young virgins are relentless

lynching today pogrom tomorrow

get some sun open the door
do something
          double life

a little milk in the tea cloud
of ordinary morning happiness
        too often invisible
        but so what you see

or find between the pages
of an old Provençal dictionary
        a letter from Cid Corman
Japanese paper   lotus leaves

the interrogative mood is the first mood

Destructive register   Followed closely   In other words insurmountable
suspicion   When we have to see what we see   I plotted out the course of my
life   Very early But I had not predicted   Everything that would have
to be endured   The pigsty   And all the rest

of course future prospective
similar to the historians'

do what you can
        as well as you can

noting in passing that like pears
        the hearts dry up

Cid's letter sent from Japan spoke
of Lorine Lorine Niedecker

she will be the heroine of the lake
because after October 5
            Chantal Akerman is its Lady

the lake is an experimental installation

the camera moves back
            retreats from the action

*Thus the strange impression   In the oldest films   We find her
aged   This cruelty of cinema   Life as it is   The late marriage
to a guy who drinks   Doesn't understand anything she writes   Harpsichord
and salted fish   They went to Copper Harbor and the Door
Peninsula   In a dream he drew a sausage*

the laws that rule
the water's motion
            are hardly known
the murderer is not transsexual
but thinks he is

the forest where the massacre took place
            is a simple wood

when the evening falls he says
the meadow saffron tastes like pepper

he says to cut down a tree
is to destroy a water filter

the set of numbers
            is based on prophetic calculation it's
musical too since all feeling
            is based on an embrace

something bilateral
him or me inside a café
            on a terrace
            facing the garden
the morning glories climbing like the clematis

Chaotic activity   Sometimes criminal   *Far from the peaceful tables*
Nighttime in this little hotel   Invisible from banks   Where he found her again
The sheets full of cigarette holes   Bottles under the bed   No room
number

I no longer amuse myself
            I no longer keep myself company
if I were alone I'd already be dead

simple discursive sampling

the tree is based on a column of its excrements

the hell of resolutions
                    dozes on the lake's back
no one sees anyone

when the 20 changes into 21 soon into 22
soon it will be Christmas all the formidable dates
unbearable procession
                    something something else
a child's outfit
                    blue running scales violet jewels
cream that has turned
a Provençal nursery scene

at the bottom of another lake
                    the voice of one Robert Filliou
in his whispered story

Since time passes   Lives unfurl   They collapse   He whispers
that everyone dies   It doesn't matter   What counts   It's that the
girls keep going in the crotch   That they sing   Have some more
strawberries   Giggle between takes

like looking for ears
                    on a frog's head
another more or less clean name
                    and the music behind

Morton Feldman returns followed by Barbara Monk

the repeated whispering

reprise without cover
                    a man at the base of the stairs
counts the beats of his heart

what you know is not important
the days go by the weeks go by
you know what your thoughts are
                              that are in my head

look closely at the poem
                              before reading it and also after

an immobile image of eternity
that's what's said
                              but nothing is immobile
especially not tears
                              fixed on each one of her cheeks

a life writing itself
without the living

a reservoir in Rome
                              as well as a cistern
or maybe it's a basin

all the empty spaces between the words
                              mean more than the words

Besides   My thoughts like my muscles   Stunted knots
*   When very close to the flowering bush   called "communal"   I squat*
at dawn and piss   Fiercely while the other   Enters
the ass   Of an impeccable and distraught blonde

nothing is missing
neither erotic boat nor declaration of love

always a double rather than a single way

an armed woman farther away
I mean visions or treasure to a
single eye

Moreover the blood between the thighs   *A vague added odor of rat*
Supposing that all readers had stayed in the cellar long enough   *The*
script goes from one end to the other   *The length of the film roll*   *Everyone*
practices imitation   *Deconstructed movement*

at the bottom of the screen and in its matinal stink
the lake more or less

emotional syncope or tear
                     several separated things

a story on each bank

here no need for bildungsroman
                     or travel narrative

sweet addition of solitudes
                     things stay the same
only the composition changes

when lower far from the lake the piano
percussive instrument added to the voice
                     instrument of the breath

a machine spitting out flames
                     free but limited in duration

the tradition of the defeated on all the banks
                    page after page

what we do with that
for example Marx and thefts of wood
                    this incident

when the document is the impression

A Poussinist on a boat   She says I see him   It's really him   Repeating
he's the one who severed the trembling hand of Poussin   Faux-
blasphemous act of retouching

no longer to say things because we think them
                    but in order not to think them anymore

a fascist use of the crowd's emotion this evening

Shut yourself up to listen to old Satie   For example the "Three
Distinguished Waltzes of a Jaded Dandy"   A simple operation   The form of
another rebellion   Useless

that things are said
                    the poor have no other choice
to be inventive or to be dead

to Augustine's dismay
                    Ambroise read soundlessly

deadly consent too
                    happens noiselessly it's the best binder
for fractures and for disconnections too

a severed hand still has five fingers

at this point in the book a brutal silence
the harmonics accented

in his general project to annotate Greek texts
Aristophanes of Byzantium introduced the comma
                              the colon and the period

maintaining that silence in Poussin
consisted of displacing point of view

                              sometimes it snows on the lake
a long traveling shot horribly slow

To those who say that Andromache's position
                              or in other words the woman on top
is 50% the cause of penis fractures

he asks humorlessly if the son of Achilles
had an asymmetrical bruise on his dick
                              Euripides didn't mention it or Virgil
nor any of the others later

The translations will often be wrong   *But that doesn't matter*
    Since "translate" is a made-up word   *For something that doesn't exist*
Intense désoeuvrement   Together with the most exhausting work   *Only*
androgyny remains   A fundamental figure   Reclaiming for the unisex
    A simple dahlia

all the ideas about coming back to life
               add madness to the arbitrary
 the bad side of things

a very big map
              to the bottom of darkness

the destructive character of those who go down there
like the wanton weirdness of others
who mix up wild rose and hawthorn
something tender and hysterical at the same time

it's my party today

what shortens and lets itself be colored
I know now I was acting
            I never stopped
as soon as I had to step outdoors

a hand cut off and thrown in the water

Interior map   *Filmed from three-quarters behind*   *Some movements*
on the surface   *the umbels*   *Humid in the gardens*   *From the morning*
The smell of coffee   *Under the lilacs*   *Where the very dear old*
whore loiters   *That we remember* *The close-ups of faces*   *How the two*
modes of stories   *Could not combine*   *No story ever*
ends   *That's what cornflowers say*   *In an Andersen fairy tale*

contemporary is he who takes
                    full in the face
the bomb for the other for all the others

beam of shadows or on to the next line
                    the utterances herald
what   a fact of the era
I also dreamed

Whatever Love is its own Allegory   Cruelty of evil which is never
banal   I didn't know I was writing about this life   All day long day   The sun
fell prey to experience   Cantos or instructions for powdered soup
*   This infinite feast in successive shadows   The subject studied exhaustively*
*   He'll rot it's fatal   The books are cold at heart   Their circular*
machine

accumulated ghosts
                    buried in mouths

my body is feminine
                    you have no idea
                    about my thoughts

splashes without constellation
                    a pale copy between us
and history relief without compiling

clouds accelerate under a low sky

pants hug the fat thighs
                    of Fassbinder smoking
he keeps them on
                    the whole length of the film

same for the infected's melancholic face

this lake like what's written
                with love or without
is it just "poets' poetry"
                the question arises

not to know it
                not to want to say it

the system had itself created
its own ways of using it
                nevertheless you could go on
to a planned-out section

red you know is beautiful
                for schizophrenics
and smelling thyme helps memory

she leans toward me
                sniffs and asks
but what day is it today

Reproduction   Spontaneous bestial   Was going to be able to be eradicated
    No longer any smell   Neither background noise nor insect flight   The naked
jumbled bodies so dazzling   That they seemed dead   Yellow latex
sign of the liver   The text itself   Had exhausted all its energies

only the children were still capable of sitting down

II

PRECIPITATE SYLLABLES

The canvas must be coarse and light in colour,
and above all, don't forget the holes. If there are no holes,
where do you expect the images to land,
what do you expect them to come through?

— FERNAND DELIGNY
FOSSILS HAVE A HARD LIFE

It's not a girl drying her tears he told her
for you to be kissed often

more like a panth

it is a tempest that blows from forge

ting in love I am a little colossus
the system had itself created the ambiguous rhyme lower down dampness of
its own ways of using it me and the opposite
to a planned-out section nevertheless you could go on
ncholic

in clear weather, with relative

e lambs' voices
ore the throat is split
's to cut down a tre
stroy a water filt

hunge
alway
of th

same for the in 'aier's s
like Vivian Maier's, pee
or Twombly's pec
ails

seem
the proper functioning

ddition of solitudes

things stay the same only

omposition changes

"exception made unless" seven y   ped all over

the same dress

torment infested with sh?

I could go bicy

stop confusing emanation

and analogy take a bath

takin?

the bottom of the screen and in its matinal stink the

nore or less

to.

that "petal" should be masculin

to have ha

like all assassins   santhemums

it get used to i.

I no longer amuse myself

I were alone I'd already be dead

I no longer keep myself compar

love will

ns are going to smash you to pieces

the one who wrote them is dead

but the notebo

for the ones who live today

was always during a storm

it was still breathing

porn star You are the subject
in the bush

to laugh

raw
is to g
c)

Get the hell out

Let's take this outside where I can take

throats Go on vacation

Drown them
&
our graves

Open our books

what is h

o dance You dance well

Why do you look at him

I had warned you

I'll take down

e hand is worth two

our clothes

astis

Emma Goldman in fine form

Make love

The sun has risen

We were dancing Yo

Who is it

care of him myself

an is its Lady

Ch

spoke of

The moon stopped in its place

Cid's fever
Lorine Loring

peel an orange or squeeze a l

in anger No
we are not angry

o longer waterlily
terdock

White rots on her feet

for example

pretty fast camellia other times just

the series

"bitter the presen

lilacs in static bunches

of lakes is "de

mended

"distancing"

s he had read B

Psychic clo

taking books and chrysanthemums

torment infested with shadows

seven years the same dress

exception made unless

its additional

partial visual object

r words is fre

with Dog-poem truth

The flower

od in

act is called

Then they smash their skulls with spades

missing a page

br

m

pe

ist

but we advance vertical

he bo

excavations

axes perspectives slow

lies the

Armed with torches carrying whips Their

oysters

class

The furies: Ferocious cocks

Unseizably bea

faces

hout a doubt to

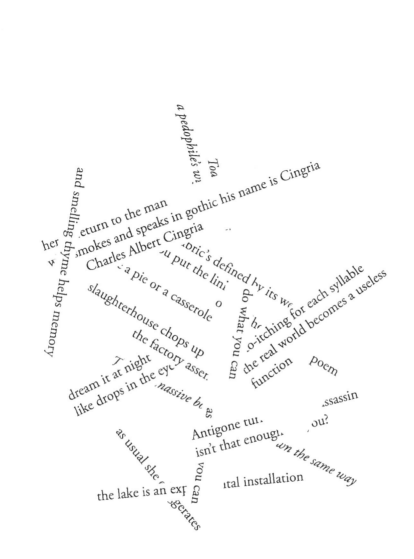

a pedophile's w.

Toa

and smelling
her ↄ
thyme helps memory

.eturn to the man
,mokes and speaks in gothic his name is Cingria
Charles Albert Cingria

ɔric's defined by its wɇ
o-itching for each syllable
the real world becomes a useless

ɔu put the lini
o
do what you can

function   poem

: a pie or a casserole
slaughterhouse chops up
the factory asser.

dream it at night
like drops in the eyɛ
.nassive bɛ as

ssassin

ɔu?

Antigone tur.
isn't that enougi.

as usual she ɕ
you can
ɔgerates

the lake is an exp
ɪtal installation

vn the same way

71

III

ONCE AND FOR NOT ALL

One does not get better because one remembers.
One remembers because one gets better.

—JACQUES LACAN

It begins in the spring. In a dream, early in the night, I clasp my hands together and crouch in the bushes. There's a photograph, I feel emotional, a little worried, because someone's talking about his shit in a paper bag where I don't see anything except sugar cubes. He says that I'm hard of hearing and thus the title of my book is given to me: *Love Is Colder than the Lake*. It's the title of a book. A book that I'm trying to write in my dream. It's in full view, open on a table, somewhere between manuscript and published version because it's already printed but I'm making endless corrections (the pages are covered with handwritten notes). The object is beautiful because it's perfectly incongruous. As if what's printed were someone else's text. Only the handwritten traces are recognizable to me. Crosshatches of color beneath certain paragraphs make it difficult to get to their meaning. What had come to my mind had before been marked on a small bit of paper, that was the explanation, but the presence of sugar hiding the shit had erased everything. Lower down I was picking yellow flowers whose names I didn't know. A yellow that doesn't exist.

In the days that follow, the dream settles in to harass me. You're going to write this book, it's your next book, here you are on the edge of it. You think, of course that's it but not with such a title! That lyrical-melodramatic, absolutely not, that title is impossible . . . It happens that I'm working on a commission from Hubert Colas, to rewrite act III of *The Seagull*, by Chekhov. He who, as he was dying, said: "I'm dying." At first, hastily, I think that this is the source of the dream transfer.

The lake is a central character. Into it pour the shadows produced by time and those who practice it. The lake is contemporary theater that remains forever to be written, which is to say, undone—that which in *The Seagull* Treplev tries to confront, and which kills him. For Treplev is confronted with the rupture of the untimely. It's not out of love for Nina that Treplev turns the gun on himself. No. For Treplev, like his uncle Sorin, is gay. It's obvious. It's not his non-love for Nina but the theatre that kills him. Every revolutionary (Lenin, Trotsky, Makhno) is a director. That's what Myerhold says.

Time passes. Buttercups scattered among the dead heads of the hydrangeas. Sudden saturation of clouds over a sky at first clear. I begin a book without a title. It's the first time in my life that I begin a book without a title. Like a recurring dream, it comes back. In another setting, with the entrance of several characters onto the scene. Like the poem, the dream deactivates the information function. It unloads and relieves. Something sparkles, and it stinks. This time it's a voice that says the title, I've lost the book, I search for it everywhere, for all its mistakes were actually quite beautiful. I'm in a train. There's a voice inside another voice. A girl is eating an apple. Rough jump in syntax. A boy asks the girl to show him her breasts. "What are you thinking about? About sex?" She responds: "About the revolution." Later I'll remember that it wasn't the girl eating the apple but the boy. She asks him if the apple was good and he responds that at twelve years old he killed his father. We see the landscape go by. The film is in black and white but at one point there's possibly a yellow dress.

A whore says: "No, I saw Johanna in a yellow dress instead." Dream-reservoir but also a trap, since "to be in the lake" exacerbates the trap even more, the expression signals a hanging, the "s" in "lakes" evoking the drawing of the rope. The lace. Chekhov is Pushkin in prose. That's what Tolstoy says. Why is Treplev gay? Because while anti-Semitism is very present in Russian literature, there are few references to homosexuality. Under Nicolas I's big stick. False, the translator of Kharms and

Klebnikov, Yvan Mignot, tells me: Pushkin has lines about a friend of his who lives in Bessarabia, he says how much he loves him, that he's ready to do anything for him except "lend him his ass." Then of course there's Lermontov. Lermontov? Did you really say Lermontov? Who drew soldiers on his manuscripts? Who died in a duel? Even if it's true, it isn't. The lake is only a hole full of water. I was told that at just the sound of my first name it went pale, all of a sudden (respiratory distress, no doubt). If you play Maeterlinck too fast, you get vaudeville. I'm at the point at which I wonder how he could have lived without that composing influence (the desire to write), morbid, variety of the fantasy of killing. I always thought he had a nice head for a killer. Girls are sometimes pretty crazy.

Trap-screen of Chekhov's lake. I should have kept in mind that in Marseille, the city where often I sleep and consequently dream, the gulls shit rats. That detail should have warned me. I had sought without finding to end up by finding, even though I had given up seeking. Treplev preceded Mandelstam, who preceded Fassbinder:

My animal, my age, who will ever be able
to look into your eyes?

Who will ever glue back together the vertebrae
of two centuries with his blood?
As for me, I spent a long time trying to understand that the form of a film depends
also on the scenes that weren't filmed, and which shadow those that were. That
phantom weight. Took weeks to end up discovering that the girl on the train who
shows her breasts comes from Fassbinder's first feature film, whose title is (bingo!)
Love Is Colder Than Death. I saw it in 1970, without subtitles. German being
totally opaque to me, a friend surprised by my amazement later "summarized"
the action. Franz aka Fassbinder, a Munich pimp, loves his whore Johanna, alias
Hanna Schygulla. He shares her with a young boy, Bruno. Thefts, murders. Franz,
preferring to work alone, has refused to join the crime syndicate. They make an
incredible trio. In the end, Johanna throws George to the cops, who kill him. On
the run, Johanna and Franz had no idea George was a traitor, paid by the syndicate.
You can never know what others want. Always love demands sacrifices, and Franz
paves the way for the Volker Schlöndorff's Brechtian character, Baal. In the credits,
the name "Straub," without "Huillet."

With the nocturnal dictation of a stolen title, I entered into a new stage of writing. As if I were myself no longer the subject of action. To write became another action. Carried by the other. Escape from the plugged-in ghost body, lit up by a side projector. Not an author. Not a poet. Rather, an acolyte, which is to say, she who accompanies in order to follow, to assist. Suppliant. The "I" becoming accomplice to a suspicious action. Guilty. She accompanies without accompaniment, like the whore who betrays. She arranges the entrance of a lake, characters in order of appearance—from Macbeth to Fassbinder—and a setting, as well as the actions that unfold in it. She takes care to let stand each word that indicates them. Auxiliary, partner, or double, she finds the poem, like the film, only after a long absence. Between fiction and reality, literature and document (the proper names almost all exist, their beauty, like their lexical force, comes from the fact that they're not words but ghosts of words), the poem was able to put its machinery into action thanks to an essential amnesia. Everything that we touch comes from the past and opens onto death for us. So only things illuminate. Far from all restoration. Half saved, half sunken.

Beneath the poem's legs is largely a matter of the survival of dead love. How to survive dead love. To write is the surest way to escape, but also—in an equally violent movement—to be caught back into it. For example, to round up. To make old images appear: register of the voice, grain of the skin, texture of the fabric. To see again. To understand. A strange shame, a true pain. How did you survive a dead love? That's the question that arises. By another love, responds the Chorus, blasé. An obtuse angle. Do we need a parenthetical statement here that would explain an entire page? Thus in a whirlwind something appears. The poem sets up its camera and films. Neither restoration nor restitution. Perhaps a form of prolongation. To try to bring back to the light the buried images (body of a man of thirty—I was fifteen—never seen again), lost, evaporated in time, he who'd now be more than eighty and who (I will learn by accident) has been dead for a quarter century. I can see his mouth and his nails, his eyelids. A scar, the trace of a knife on the first joint of his index finger. The smell of mild tobacco. He loves the heroine in a quarry, gets her pregnant. The very one who (I'll learn much later) should have impressed a poet named du Bouchet. In full daylight. It's this sun on white limestone I was thinking of at the moment I insert the laminary sticks, and when I discovered the black blood inside my thighs. I was imagining the miniscule bones of the fetus in the palm of my hand. With terror, imagining them as little game pieces. The abortion was a crime, the still-child disposing of her own child doubly dripping with crime.

How we stayed still for the winter, immobile, interlaced at the foot of a tree in the little pine forest where I'd find him. That force which hurried us into an embrace and the silence while our mouths searched for each other's. An almost painful breathing of language and the impossibility of speech. A singular experience, outside of all meaning, where the very limits of sex or of sentiment were pushed offscreen. I remember the noise of the wind in the trees over our heads. The unformed form of the wind's movement just over our bodies, he clothed and me naked, wrapped in his coat, and ultimately his penis buried in me. The obsolescence of such a memory, since the only one who could share it with me is dead, that scandal attached itself to the places where the action took place, that never would the secret be revealed, that having learned upon adulthood (five years later) that he had fathered another child, this one real, in the end I gave up the plan of crossing the ocean to America to kill him. A model of the ante- pulverized by the post-, the heroine from then on inhabiting a half-dead body and surviving for a time only by relentless use of sex and books. Thus the fact that it's upon this indestructible experience that all of her amorous adventures would be constructed, like in the novels she would read. Sometimes at night I awaken, believing I recognize the noise of the wind in the trees. But no, it's cars along the boulevard.

To try to say it, impracticable for a long time and all the way until this actual December evening (a form of micrological exploration), appears imaginable for the first time. Spoken of my past. I can say it, it's upon this drama that all my forces are built, the preceding pages, a film upon another film, a recitative crossed by a lake, other characters. For whatever the words concerning this love are, they occupy a hole that I'd have on the tip of my tongue and that would remain there until my death. The lake's water filled the hole. The lake inhabits the book. That which I read in writing it. For the words are turned away from the page. They're silences between the words that have become the sites for another casting. Another film. Outside the destruction of language has begun. "Procedure of distancing" replaces "Measures of expulsion," "Different success," "Failure of schools," "Plan for saving jobs," "Group layoffs" . . . death encroaches. Like the shame of surviving in a privileged world in a world that is strangling itself. The instrument I use is, remains, ill-suited, because it advances by fragments. A ceaseless stopping is the poem's rhythm, and introduces successions of pauses like Polaroids, time clinking with motifs illustrating the preparation and the repetition of murders. Past and to come. Individual or mass. The demarcating line between prose and poetry is continually moving. Something deep and determined in the use of a cold technique. Today, what is important to me is combination. Thoreau was right. Experience is in the hands and in the head. The heart has no experience. The poem knows about all of us for much longer than we do. And because it still burns in a devastated world, love is colder than the lake.

CHARACTERS IN ORDER OF APPEARANCE

MACBETH (*see* SHAKESPEARE)

EMMA GOLDMAN (1869-1940)

ORPHEUS

CHRISTOPH WILLIBALD GLUCK (1714-1787)

MEPHISTOPHELES

SNOW WHITE

DONATIEN ALPHONSE FRANÇOIS DE SADE (1740-1814)

WILLIAM SHAKESPEARE (1564-1616)

MOLLOY (*see* BECKETT)

LOUIS ZUKOFSKY (1904-1978)

LORINE NIEDECKER (1903-1970)

ALOIS ALZHEIMER (1864-1915)

THE FURIES

VIVIAN MAIER (1926-2009)

FAUST

ADOLF HITLER (1889-1945)

CATULLUS (84 BC-54 BC)

CHRISTOPHER MARLOWE (1564-1593)

CY TWOMBLY (1928-2011)

DARIUS I

FRIEDRICH HÖLDERLIN (1770-1843)

BERTOLT BRECHT (1898-1956)

STÉPHANE MALLARMÉ (1842-1898)

JOCASTA

CHARLES-ALBERT CINGRIA (1883-1954)

ALIX CLÉO ROUBAUD (1952-1983)

CREON

ANTIGONE

CID CORMAN (1924-2004)
CHANTAL AKERMAN (1950-2015)
ROBERT FILLIOU (1926-1987)
MORTON FELDMAN (1926-1987)
BARBARA MONK (1953-)
KARL MARX (1818-1883)
NICOLAS POUSSIN (1594-1665)
ERIK SATIE (1866-1925)
SAINT AUGUSTINE (354-430)
SAINT AMBROISE (340-397)
ARISTOPHANES OF BYZANTIUM (257 BC-180 BC)
HECTOR (SON OF PRIAM)
EURIPIDES (485 BC-406 BC)
VIRGIL (70 BC-19 BC)
RAINER WERNER FASSBINDER (1945-1982)
HANNA SCHYGULLA (1943-)

Not every character listed is really a character.

ACKNOWLEDGMENTS

Excerpts from this book have appeared in *Asymptote, The Stinging Fly*, and on the Action Books website. Grateful thanks to the editors of these publications.

Previous translations of epigraphs are drawn from *Camering: Fernand Deligny on Cinema and the Image*, edited by Marlon Miguel, translated by Sarah Moses (Amsterdam: Amsterdam University Press, 2022, p. 135) and from Jacques Lacan's *Écrits: A Selection*, translated by Bruce Fink (New York: Norton, 2002, p. 249).

Some of the translation work, and the teaming of Riggs and Turner, was done during the Tamaas Translation Seminar.

The translators wish to thank Kit Schluter, not only for the formatting of the book, but for the arrangement of the collages and suggestions in the content of the book's translation.

LILIANE GIRAUDON was born in the South of France in 1946. She continues to live and work in Marseille, and her writing is inseparable from the place, shaped by the vibrant community of poets and writers and artists Giraudon has herself shaped, as well as by the city's gritty and diverse cosmopolitanism. Giraudon's many books have, since 1982, been primarily published by France's P.O.L. editions. Giraudon has also been instrumental as an editor for influential reviews such as *Banana Split*, *Action Poétique*, and *If*. She performs and collaborates widely, including with Nanni Balestrini, Henri Deluy, Jean-Jacques Viton, and many others. Two of her books, *Fur* and *Pallaksch, Pallaksch* were published in English by Sun & Moon Press in 1992 and 1994, respectively.

LINDSAY TURNER is the author of the poetry collections *Songs & Ballads* (2018) and *The Upstate* (2023). She has twice received French Voices awards for her translations from the French, which include books of poetry and philosophy by Stéphane Bouquet, Souleymane Bachir Diagne, Anne Dufourmantelle, Ryoko Sekiguchi, and others. She is Assistant Professor of English and Creative Writing at Case Western Reserve University in Cleveland, Ohio.

SARAH RIGGS is a poet and multivalent artist. Her most recent book *The Nerve Epistle* appeared in 2021. Translation is one of her arts, for which she received a Griffin prize with Etel Adnan, and Best Translated Book Award, also for Adnan's *Time* (Nightboat, 2019). Riggs lives in Brooklyn, after many years in Paris.

NIGHTBOAT BOOKS

Nightboat Books, a nonprofit organization, seeks to develop audiences for writers whose work resists convention and transcends boundaries. We publish books rich with poignancy, intelligence, and risk. Please visit nightboat.org to learn about our titles and how you can support our future publications.

The following individuals have supported the publication of this book. We thank them for their generosity and commitment to the mission of Nightboat Books:

Kazim Ali • Anonymous (8) • Mary Armantrout • Jean C. Ballantyne • Thomas Ballantyne • Bill Bruns • John Cappetta • V. Shannon Clyne • Ulla Dydo Charitable Fund • Photios Giovanis • Amanda Greenberger • Vandana Khanna • Isaac Klausner • Shari Leinwand • Anne Marie Macari • Elizabeth Madans • Martha Melvoin • Caren Motika • Elizabeth Motika • The Leslie Scalapino - O Books Fund • Robin Shanus • Thomas Shardlow • Rebecca Shea • Ira Silverberg • Benjamin Taylor • David Wall • Jerrie Whitfield & Richard Motika • Arden Wohl • Issam Zineh

This book is made possible, in part, by grants from the New York City Department of Cultural Affairs in partnership with the City Council and the New York State Council on the Arts Literature Program.